TESTIMONIALS ___

Frank's book on soccer culture is a brilliant, insightful dive into the soul of the game, written by someone who's lived it fully. As a dear friend and once-revered opponent, Frank brings a rare mix of warmth, wit, and hard-earned wisdom to every page. His deep knowledge and love for soccer make this book a must-read for anyone who wants to understand not just how the game is played— but why it matters."

—Jeremy Gunn, Stanford University men's soccer head coach, three-time NCAA DI champion, NCAA DII title winner at Fort Lewis College, and NCAA Final Four qualifier with UNC Charlotte

■ ■ ■ ■ ■

Coach Frank (or 'Uncle Frank,' as we called him in our program) has been a transformational mentor for me, helping to guide not only my soccer program, but my personal growth as a person. He is my #1 truth-teller— even when I don't want to hear it! His direct and honest leadership style inspires everyone around him to rise to their highest potential—on and off the field. More than a coach, he's an incredible human being whose love for dogs and unwavering dependability reveal the depth of his character. This book is a reflection of the values he brings to every team, every conversation, and every life he touches."

—Ross Duncan, University of Central Arkansas men's head soccer coach, first client of Best Day Ever Consulting, standout assistant coach at the University of Vermont, and top men's soccer athlete at Oregon State University, with a coaching license from US Soccer and UEFA

■ ■ ■ ■ ■

Frank knows how to build teams, create a strong culture, and have success. This read is for anyone who wants to build a team and live with purpose. Frank has been a championship coach for five decades. This book is one of the most valuable tools any young coach can read. I recommend you adopt the core covenants and experience what it's like to go deep into a winning culture."

—Dr. Dan Freigang, renowned sport psychologist who worked with: FC Bayern Munich, the Stanford University men's soccer team, UNC Charlotte, Fort Lewis College, University of Central Arkansas, and other successful college and professional teams

■ ■ ■ ■ ■

I was very fortunate to play for Frank at UNC Charlotte. His love for the game, pursuit of excellence, and his ability to get the best out of his players are three characteristics

UNDERDOGS TO DAWGS TO WINNERS

THE LESS-TRAVELED TRAIL

FRANK KOHLENSTEIN

ISBN: 978-1-956464-65-8

First Edition 2025

This publication is intended to provide accurate information on the subject matter covered. It is sold with the understanding that neither the author nor the publisher offers legal, investment, accounting, medical, or other professional advice. The author and publisher make no representations or warranties regarding the accuracy or completeness of the contents and expressly disclaim any implied warranties of merchantability or fitness for a particular purpose. No warranties may be extended by sales representatives or materials. Professional consultation is recommended as individual circumstances vary. Neither the author nor the publisher shall be liable for any damages, including but not limited to loss of profit, incidental, or consequential damages.

Published by BrightRay Publishing
https://brightray.com/

that I have taken with me—first as a professional player and now as a professional coach. Frank is a winner in every sense of the word. I am extremely thankful for our time together."

—Jon Busch, professional coach
and 20+ year professional,
UNC Charlotte Hall of Fame Member,
NCAA DI All-American, and MLS Goalkeeper of the Year

■ ■ ■ ■ ■

Frank Kohlenstein is one of the best minds in the game. He possesses the ability to see small details in your team that others miss. Frank can and will make your team better."

—Robbie Church, Duke University women's soccer
head coach (2001–2024), retired as the winningest
coach in Duke women's soccer history, with four NCAA
Final Four appearances

■ ■ ■ ■ ■

I have shared my soccer experience with Frank as a player, an assistant coach, and a colleague from college to the pro ranks. In all of these roles and at all of these levels, I have witnessed Frank's methods. They work."

—Kevin Fickes, a former collegiate and pro soccer
athlete, now one of the most successful coaches in
NCAA women's soccer

This book is dedicated to Jenna, Schatz, Silky, Chloe, Jiggy, Bozeman, Aussie, Foxey, Tuke, Digsby, Scarlet, Daja, Nena, Kazoo, Razoo, Bubbster, Cabbie, Grack, Arbuckles, Tewinot, Driggs, and Grey Ghost—they made every day special and were always glad to see me, no matter how the team was doing.

Also, to Deb, who has never let results get in the way of her support and has made me want to be a better human each day, to follow her lead.

You ain't run far enough to say
It ain't gonna get better.

—"Hey Mama" by Nathaniel Rateliff is a song that embodies the philosophy I have as a coach and the expectations of productivity and attitude I have for myself and my athletes. It exhibits the standard we should all follow.

TABLE OF CONTENTS _____

FOREWORD

Frank Kohlenstein is more than just a soccer coach—he's a builder. He has built championship-winning teams, soccer programs from the ground up, and cultures that create bonds bigger than the sport. But most importantly, he's a builder of character. Hard work, consistency, integrity, and respect were not just values written on a wall in the locker room, they were the high standard he held himself and everyone around him to.

I've known Frank for over two decades. I first met him at his summer soccer camp at the Colorado School of Mines when I was ten years old, and then later played for him at Mines. I leaned on him as a mentor and friend throughout my professional sports career and still do to this day. My main takeaway from our 20+ years together is his phrase: "Winners Always Win." He didn't mean in the scoreboard sense, but in the way you show up—giving it your all, every time, in everything you do. Through that lens, Frank taught me to be a better soccer player, student, friend, leader, and ultimately, a better person.

This book is filled with those practical and powerful lessons, developed through lived experience and more than six decades of success at the highest levels. It's about building teams, habits, mindsets, and relationships that endure. Whether you're a coach, player, or someone simply trying to create something meaningful, I guarantee you'll find something here that speaks to you.

—Tesho Akindele, four-time All-American men's soccer athlete at Colorado School of Mines, highest ranked men's soccer DII draft pick in MLS history, MLS Rookie of the Year, with a nine-year career at FC Dallas and Orlando City of the MLS

FINDING THE TRAILHEAD _____

The ritual was always the same: unpack our minimal belongings at the conventional lodgings on base, then hurry out to the quad to find kids my age. Growing up in a military family, we were always relocating—always packing and unpacking. There was a singular truth no matter where we landed though: Kids were pigeonholed based on their parents' rank. Even housing on base was assigned based on rank and family size.

The exception was when us kids met up to play sports. It was a level playing field, one that brought everyone together. There was no rank, no personal histories—just our childish resilience to skin our knees and keep playing. You could earn respect for how you played. Those were some of my favorite times, even when the facilities were less than ideal. When I played, I wasn't worrying about where we were or where my dad's next assignment would take us. My focus was on making the right moves to score points.

I was always a little out of my element as a kid. Not only from the frequent moving, but because my natural playmate was my brother Don, who was three years older than me. Ever the underdog among my brother and his friends, I learned to play smart, to fight harder for the win, and to develop those areas my older teammates and opponents would not. It was a real confidence booster and came in handy later when I started coaching—training underdog teams was like looking in a mirror! As we said at the University of North Carolina–Charlotte during my years there: To be fit and to defend in areas that other teams did not emphasize, but as underdogs, allowed us to become champions. Later, this became the core covenant that I would use with many teams.

Since I was about 10 years old, I wanted to work with sports in some capacity. To me, being a physical education teacher looked like a great way to live. You could be outside, moving around, playing games, and encouraging people to try their best. It sounded infinitely better than being stuck in a cubicle all day. As I entered high school, the counselors and teachers wanted me to consider other options. I was a high achiever, and they thought I should become a doctor or lawyer. But I had made up my mind when I was 10 and saw no reason to change it. Funnily enough, it's that unwavering resolve and determination that defined my 40+ years as a coach.

My first coaching experience was theoretically low-stakes: At 17, I stepped in to coach my sister's summer pre-teen softball team so they could play in the league. I didn't know much about coaching yet, but I intimately knew sports, and with this coaching gig, I was ready to be on the other side of the field.

With everything sports-related, I put my whole heart into the job. You would think I led the girls' team with compassion—that I *inspired*. But if asked, my sisters, Betsy and Karen, would probably say otherwise. They would accuse me of pushing them too hard—and, of course, they're right. In my mind, it would have been a disservice to let them skate by. I had high expectations because I *knew* they were capable of more—and I demanded it.

Coaching boils down to strategy and people skills. You have to make the right moves and motivate players to become better at every turn. As I say: BEST PLAY + BEST WAY = BEST DAY! The particulars of this may be more intricate, but having this mindset sets the foundation for success.

As a junior college student, I got to play organized soccer when Charles Pulley, a physical education professor, agreed to coach us if we rounded up enough athletes. He did it for the sole reason of giving us the opportunity to play. Later, when Pulley was on sabbatical, I coached the JC team, and that was a springboard for other soccer opportunities.

Not long after my college graduation, I ended up in Niceville, Florida, teaching science, math, and PE at the junior high school. I enjoyed the work and kept busy by also coaching the school's football and track teams.

Coaching took me in other directions too. I always ended up either (1) filling someone else's shoes and trying to build on their legacy, or (2) inheriting a program that was new or needed an overhaul. No matter my starting point, I was always learning from other coaches and other sports to become a better leader.

After Okaloosa Walton, I made my way to the University of South Carolina–Spartanburg (USCS). It was my first time coaching at a four-year institution. They didn't have a soccer team before I got there, so it was almost like the team and I grew together. Once again, I found myself the underdog in a classic one-man show—I had no support staff and limited resources. But that's how I thrived. I was learning how to make the most of any situation. The team was a lot like a family; sometimes I was the nice, fun uncle, and other times I was the strict, mean one. At the core, I was always trying to be a role model, living the life I was asking my players to live on and off the practice field. My wife, Deb, was a big part of making all of us a family—she and our dogs were reigning favorites with every team. Deb could easily teach a course on how to be a coach's partner! I worked with the team on being able to count on one another.

Even with our lack of resources, we believed we could win with hard work. The team loved to train hard and compete hard, and let me tell you, it paid off. Three years later, we made it to the Final Four three seasons in a row. Later, it became the core covenant: Control the controllable.

Soccer is a lot like chess in that you have to think several steps ahead. There's no stopping for huddles like in football, and there's no prescribed gameplay like in basketball; you have to train the athletes to play on their feet and make those snap decisions without your guidance. This, of course, is after training your team to work together on the best options to handle different game scenarios. They have to be leaders on the field and show up ready to learn in practice. A coach with a strong training program is vital for a soccer team since they're required to make the decisions during matches. It's part of the reason I started my business, Best Day

Ever Consulting, which answers the question on every coach's mind: How can we maximize human potential, team potential, and organizational potential?

I asked this question when I first joined the University of Central Arkansas Purple Bears men's soccer team as a consultant working with Head Coach Ross Duncan, his staff, and their sports psychologist, Dr. Dan Freigang. Standing in front of the team, I gave them the enlightening kind of pep talk that inspires: YOU CAN WIN! We weren't winners—not at that point. We were underdogs, but I knew we could win. Later, Dr. Freigang told me that it was the first time a coach had ever told that group that they could overcome their disadvantage, maximize their human potential, and make a name for themselves. When I first arrived, the team was 0–6. Working with the Purple Bears, I challenged them to:

- Push their ceiling
- Understand their role within the program
- Believe in themselves and their teammates
- Continue to improve their character and culture

After our work together, they won the Missouri Valley Conference and an NCAA tournament bid for the very first time. Maximum potential was achieved through best play—all because Ross was willing to seek solutions and work together to help the team! This is a trail few coaches would take. It's a coach's job to find a way, even when it's a path few are strong enough to travel.

Over the years, I have coached many sports. Any time a coach left, I stepped in to help until the school or organization hired someone new. It was a part of a learning curve, but I focused on player development and training, culture-building, and developing leadership skills—making the concepts manageable by breaking tasks into simple, concise actions to achieve success. My extensive coaching experiences taught me how to adapt to different sports and work with a variety of athletes. I knew that, as a coach, I could teach people life lessons through the sport: Believe in yourself, work together, set high standards, interact with empathy, and overcome life's hurdles.

Each coach I know has their own list of goals, some of which are solely focused on the outcomes, but there's more to the job than a final score—winners always win, even if it's not reflected on the scoreboard. They get better every day. Being on a team is a means to teach people to improve their lives, deliver lessons, and navigate the joys and hardships of life. Some coaches teach the technical skills and leave it at that, but the best coaches leave a legacy of player development and an incredible culture. A legacy isn't built by accident or without hard work. All of us are a coach, a leader, or an athlete for at least one person. With this responsibility, there's the need for continuous growth. The chapters ahead can aid in your journey to becoming a better coach, leader, or athlete, reaching maximum potential. It starts with a clear philosophy— one that guides every decision, every practice, and every athlete you mentor. This philosophy is the start of your trip on the trail less traveled: Keep your eyes open for inspiration to improve your team and organization.

The Path Isn't Straight

Much like a soccer match, the lessons in this book have been hard won. They aren't picture-perfect, but they're real. From my early coaching days to the wisdom of experience, I've learned that the beautiful game is all-encompassing. It demands peak athleticism—coaches and players alike have to be prepared for every catastrophe. A good header can set you up for a strong attack, but it takes solid technical work to finish the job.

CHAPTER ONE

MAKE IT HAPPEN

I first want to preface this story by saying that the rules and expectations back in the day were not the same as they are now. Now that you're adequately intrigued, one of the most memorable moments while I was coaching at USCS happened when we were traveling for an away game. We boarded this brand-new bus, thinking how lucky we were to enjoy fancy transportation, only for it to break down on the road. We weren't even close to our destination! The team and I spent five hours waiting for that freaking bus to be fixed. It caused such a delay that we didn't make it to our hotel until 2 a.m. Despite the circumstances, we showed up the next morning and went all-in for the match, pulling a win.

On our way home, the bus broke down . . . *again*. Even riding the high from our win, we were exhausted, and as the repairs dragged on, the boys and I started to worry that we wouldn't make it back in time for classes and work on Monday. So, I walked to a U-Haul and rented a box truck big enough to fit us and our gear. The team settled in good-naturedly, and we made it home in one piece.

For a different coach, this could have been a nightmare situation, but my team kept good spirits. They even pulled out a wiffleball and played at a gas station to pass the time away. They found the positive in the situation. Some people will say that a team is made on the field or during a teeth-clencher of a game, but from my decades as a coach, I can tell you this: Teams are made on buses, planes, trains, and in hotels. It's the unscripted parts that they remember. And that's why, as a coach, you need an impenetrable philosophy to guide you through the planned *and* the unexpected. It took me a while to craft my personal philosophy into words. At the center of it, the foundation that supports my five-pronged philosophy is Frank's Pyramid of Joy.

On the bottom lies casual *fun*, then *happiness*, and at the top, true *joy*. The *fun* consists of low-stakes moments—think bowling, going for a nice walk—that sort of enjoyable, brief time. Then comes *happiness*, when you're drinking coffee with your partner or cuddling with your pet. This *happiness* is less fleeting and feeds something in your soul. Finally, at the top of the pyramid is *joy*. *Joy* is when you have faced and overcome challenges and put in the work to reach the pinnacle. Seeing my team win a hard-fought game or closing down the season with an unexpected victory is the kind of true joy we all chase in life. For years, I embraced this Pyramid of Joy, but it wasn't until five years ago that I finally shared it with my athletes.

Pyramid of Joy: The Shelter Dogs Endure

For the past seven years, I have been volunteering at Foothills Animal Shelter (FAS) in Golden, Colorado. My time there puts me at the top of my Pyramid of Joy. It is a good facility for animals of all kinds, with wonderful people working and volunteering there. Since I have been spending hundreds of hours there, I have learned a great deal from the fantastic vets, staff, and techs there, but the greatest inspiration has come from the shelter dogs.

These pups of all ages have come into the shelter as strays, surrenders, found dogs, or rescues from possibly bad situations. These dogs are teachers of life lessons that we could all benefit from:

- **Be Ready for a Great Day:** Each day, when someone walks in, the dogs and their body language say, "Hey! Hey! Let's have a great day." The pups are ready to make the most of the day ahead—they are not worried about what happened yesterday or what's going to happen tomorrow, only focused on having the best day that they can. Imagine how much better our days would be if we started each day in the same positive way.

- **Be 100 Percent Committed to What You're Doing:** When these pups go for a walk, they are completely immersed in it. They focus on whatever they're doing—eating, barking, playing—to enjoy it to the fullest. Think about how much more we would get out of our days and even our lives if we gave our focus to one thing at a time.

- **Be Ready to Make New Friends:** Being in a new and unfamiliar environment, some of the dogs can become intimidated. But most are ready to open up their hearts to meet and greet new dogs and people, as well as the possibility of a new life. Like these dogs, we can enrich our lives by staying open to new connections and friendships along our journey.

- **Bounce Back from the Bad Stuff:** Shelter dogs often go through tough times, but they remarkably come back from challenges. They don't let the bad stuff or past pain keep them from finding love and happiness. These pups keep moving forward, finding ways to bounce back. If we could recover from our own setbacks the way they do, we could rediscover the joy of living and loving.

- **Find Joy:** These dogs wag their tails, have a twinkle in their eyes, and jump for joy in finding the simplest pleasures in their day. This is a great lesson; they look for joy all the time. I hope all of us strive to reach every level of my Pyramid of Joy to appreciate the simple wonders that are all around us. If you're struggling to see what joy looks like, visit your local shelter!

Our precious Daja was a 10-year-old, 80-pound pitbull from the Foothills Animal Shelter when we fostered her for Thanksgiving. Pretty soon, Deb and I decided that all we needed for Christmas was to add Daja to our family permanently. We did so knowing full well we wouldn't have a long time together, but those three years brought us endless joy.

I've always had guiding principles. I can remember the mantra from one of my first years at Spartanburg: No Regrets, No Excuses. It encouraged the players to give their all for the challenge at hand and find solutions for any limitations—and it empowered me to devote the energy and time needed to bring out the best in my athletes. After a loss in the semi-finals, we added "Never Surrender" to the team's philosophy. In those early days, as I coached with a variety of athletes in different sports, I collected nuggets of knowledge to guide my work, but it wasn't until my job at Central Arkansas that I refined them into five cohesive covenants:

- Be All-In
- Train Like an Underdog, Compete Like a Champion
- Purple Bears Take Care of Purple Bears
- Control the Controllables
- #5, Do It Now

The Purple Bears of Arkansas lived and breathed this collective philosophy, and the results of our efforts speak for themselves: In just four years as head coach, we went to three ASUN Championship matches and produced a dozen All-Conference performers. That success took time and effort, starting with embracing this philosophy.

Be All-In

The best in any sport or industry are the people who go all-in, no holding back or second-guessing. Easy to say, but certainly not easy to do. For athletes, this entails being present and prepared for practices and games. I ask them: What does your 100 percent look like today? Usually, it means getting the right sleep, eating properly, and staying hydrated in order to play their best, but it could also mean them committing their all to a new training program. For the Purple Bears, the student-athletes who fully "bought in" saw the most progress, getting better and making efforts that helped the whole team succeed together. That said, a team is only as strong as its least bought-in member. Whatever the team has decided to do, every athlete needs to go all-in. Otherwise, they become a flat tire, dragging everyone to a halt.

As a coach, the all-in mindset is no different. One of my former athletes, Jon Busch—a UNC Charlotte Hall of Famer who played 22 years of pro ball before becoming a coach—spoke to me and said that it wasn't until he became a coach that he realized how important it is for the staff to live the way they ask the players to live. Their committed mindset, dedication, and enthusiasm set the example. Why would a player respect or listen to a coach who's sitting on the sidelines, punctuating his commands with a beer or a cigarette? The double standard would smother any motivation and commitment the athletes have, no matter how "genius" the coach may seem. As a leader, it's my job to step up, be dedicated to the work, and remain present for the team.

Many assistant coaches don't realize the work that goes into the head coach role. The team is on your mind 24/7, all 365 days a year. Some assistant or specialized coaches will punch out for the day, saying, "I'm not taking calls after 7 p.m.," but life doesn't only happen from 9 a.m. to 7 p.m. At the college level, parents are trusting us with their kids. It would be a disservice to tap out at the end of the day without remembering that fact.

Train Like an Underdog, Compete Like a Champion

The best teams I've worked with are the ones who start as underdogs. They have fewer resources and apparent disadvantages, but all that means is they're willing to outwork and outdo the competition. These teams have something to prove, and on some level, don't we all? You can use this as a driving force and continual motivation. Underdogs are willing to do the extras: become more fit, squeeze in extra reps on defending, train their free kicks, and develop the fundamentals.

At the University of Central Arkansas (UCA), the door to the training pitch was plastered with a sign: "Train Like an Underdog." On the other side, another door led to the match field with the sign, "Compete like a champion." This was in our "soccer house." You read that right: It was an old ranch house that encompassed garage locker rooms and had space for the coaching offices. Now, I could have commiserated—gotten hung up on our lack of fancy facilities—but instead, my staff and I leaned into it.

We turned the soccer house into a place players wanted to be. With a fully-equipped kitchen, we cooked for the athletes—or they would cook for each other—and we would gather in the family room to connect. I took up a near-permanent residence at the kitchen table with a cup of tea or coffee. Players and staff alike knew that if I wasn't at home and we weren't practicing, they could find me at the table. I made myself available to the team and was rewarded with a close-knit group who could face down our competitors and come out on top.

The mindset of an underdog is that they believe there is a way to accomplish any goal—even if it means taking a path different from what everyone else is using. I've consistently coached at schools with fewer staff, less money in scholarships, and outdated or limited equipment and facilities. Instead of allowing that chip on my shoulder to stop my progress, I've let it be a reason to push harder. Always looking to take the next step to a higher level and pursue higher standards on the field and off. Do not make excuses—find a way *together*. Seek to turn underdogs into *dawgs*!

As a consultant, I worked to galvanize the Generals to optimize their underdog label. On March 20, 2018, I headed out from Golden, Colorado, to work with the Sheridan College soccer program. It was a junior college headed by a young coach, Coach Tim Starr, who was doing the work solo. No assistant coach or resources. He only had his wife, Harmony, a former soccer player, to give him feedback. Thankfully, Tim was ready to let go of the reins a bit and adopt a growth mindset—both for himself and for his program to improve.

I met the team for training before the sun was even up. The turf field was coated with a thin layer of frost, and everyone was eager to get started with their first training after spring break. The Sheridan team had already played one spring match and was looking forward to their second match versus a DII opponent. In the first session, I mainly observed to see the strengths and weaknesses of the team and how the team responded to Tim's training ideas. The practice ended with some 6v6 action. Tim had a growth mindset and was open to talking through every inch of the training plan. We spent the rest of the day exchanging ideas about what his student athletes needed, how to help them reach their potential, what to cover in our training sessions, and how to get the team involved in their leadership.

On day two, we focused on raising the intensity of our attack by committing numbers forward while also emphasizing the importance of getting those numbers back to defend. We finished with a 7v7, working on match management, such as exercising discipline and being unselfish. Day three followed the same strategy to prepare for the next match.

Match day started with a three-hour drive, but before long, we were on a turf field fighting 20 mph winds in a tough match. Tim Starr adapted to the situation, and by the end, only five players were in their original positions—with two reserve goalkeepers stepping in as forwards—because of injury and lack of numbers. In the end, the team earned a hard-fought draw. It was an underdog situation, but through unselfish discipline, the Sheridan Generals were galvanized to get better.

Purple Bears Take Care of Purple Bears

We've all heard "there's no 'I' in team"; this takes that notion and makes it actionable. Every single player is on the team for a reason. Each brings their skills and weaknesses. The last thing I want, as a coach, is to have a team that lets its players fall. If someone needs a ride, a teammate should step up. Perhaps some of them are taking a particularly difficult class—sounds like the perfect time to set up a study group. A strong team is one that uplifts its members and demands accountability from all. Whenever I hear a player say, "That's not what we do here," or something to that effect, I know my culture is taking root in a positive way. We need to expect the best from each other and give a nudge or a stern talking-to if someone is coming up short. Whether it's a teammate needing help on the field or off, we are there for each other, be they Rifle Boyz, Niners, Diggers, or Purple Bears. When you're taking care of each other, you build a bond to hold each other accountable and grow as a team.

As you are building a program, never lose sight of the importance of looking after each other—only then can you reach your fullest potential. As a coach, it's down to you to set the tone and ensure your athletes work as the team they're meant to be.

Control the Controllable

Seasoned coaches will know just how hopeless it is to anticipate every scenario. There is so much beyond our control, from resources provided to scholarships offered to the quality of the competition. So, what do we do?

Some would sit back and take it easy, ready with a pile of excuses for a poor job.

The coaches who are committed to their craft know that this is when the real work happens: You focus your energy on the elements within your reach. You *can* control your attitude. Your training plan. How hard you're willing to work. The pep talk you give the team before a big game. Each of these can have a profound impact not only on morale but on the results of the game. The truest test of this covenant is a game with a referee you disagree with. You can't control the calls, even the ones you find unfair, but you *can* control your reaction. Sometimes, the situation gets heated, but as a coach, you need to find the best way to show the team you're standing with them. They deserve as much.

When I inherited the Purple Bears soccer team at Central Arkansas, I knew we were underdogs compared to other DI programs. We weren't going to have the resources of Wake Forest or Southern Methodist University. I could have chosen sleepless nights of worrying about those facts, but that's not what it means to be a coach. I signed up to do the best I could with what I had there. That meant hard work, turning the soccer house into a true family space for the team. Recognize the resources you have, and make the most of them.

At the athlete level, Control the Controllables feeds into Be All-In. I expect our team to show up on time, be ready to work hard, have a positive attitude, and come with an open mind. Notice that the list has nothing to do with talent or resources. Their willingness to get better and learn is the best resource we have to work with, and, more importantly, it's within our control.

5, Do It Now

Life is busy. We all know how easy it is to procrastinate and make excuses. A student-athlete is no exception. They're being asked to give the team their all while juggling classwork and some semblance of a social life. There are a lot of demands on their time and many distractions. This becomes a program-killer when excuses replace action. I could list a hundred excuses, but it doesn't change the facts: If I wait until two weeks before pre-season starts to get in shape, I won't be ready to Be All-In. I certainly won't be fit enough to work out beside my players. It's easy to put off responsibilities, and without proper attention, that procrastination can become part of how we think.

In fact, "Do It Now" became such a pillar for our team that the players and I would say a quick "Hey man, number 5" as a necessary check-in to keep each other accountable.

Define Your Philosophy

No one accomplishes the exceptional alone. A philosophy is no different. Every team and athlete in Spartanburg, Charlotte, Golden, and Conway, and every coach I have worked with or competed against, have helped form my philosophy. My grounding, five-covenant philosophy and Pyramid of Joy pay tribute to my decades as a coach and player. They're influenced by experience, mentors, and athletes. My advice to any new coach is to take nuggets of wisdom from every leader and teacher you've been around. Pull from their ideas and make them yours.

One of my inspirations was Charles Pulley, my coach at junior college. He'd be the first to admit that he didn't know much about the technical side of soccer. But that man was still a gifted coach. How? Most of all, it was because he was a man to respect, and he knew how to *connect* with people. Charles could inspire us and get us to work as a team. The man put in so many hours—completely unpaid—just to give us the opportunity to play. Talk about leading—he was utterly driven by a passion for coaching and enhancing the experiences of the students he mentored. With our limited resources, a unified team was the only fighting chance we had against competitors. Charles was an influential reason for why I finally decided to become a coach.

I also want to caution any coach to recognize how much there is to learn. From my vantage point, many of the most humble coaches are ones with decades of experience. The newer coaches get a few wins and strut around feeling untouchable. I was no different. By my third year at USCS, we made it to the Final Four, and my attitude shifted to "I got this thing down." You have to keep working every day. What happened in the past doesn't carry over unless you are working at moving forward. When you think you "have it," you stop getting better, and I realized that complacency will leave you a step (or several) behind your competition. At every turn, every game, you need to be ready to tweak your approach and continue to grow. There are some areas that are constant principles, but most times, you need to be ready to change, to grow, and to elevate. Always look for ways to move yourself and your program forward. Get better every day!

This is especially true after losses, which is a key time to become better as a team and program. Everyone knows there is work to be done. They have big ears and open minds. It all starts with the coach and staff being accountable: What can we do better in preparation and training? This approach allows the team to follow your lead and uses disappointment to motivate them to move forward. Losses should inspire you to work harder than every athlete on your team, starting with intentionally crafting and practicing your philosophy.

Whether it's a usual training session or an unexpected situation during a match, it's your philosophy that keeps you from faltering—so build it, practice it, and live it. Only with a strong foundational philosophy can you build an enduring culture and, therefore, a successful program.

CHAPTER TWO

YOU HAVE NOT RUN FAR ENOUGH

A coach is never guaranteed to inherit a successful program; as a matter of fact, that's usually why you have come in—to fix a program—and sometimes, it needs to be built from the ground up. Such was the case when I began coaching at the Colorado School of Mines. As a premier engineering school, the players had overloaded schedules and treated soccer like a hobby. There were a few players who were passionate about being college soccer players—but not nearly enough to carry the program. No chance in hell I'm letting that slide! Each year, we converted more players to the joy of being a committed member of the program. I added extras to the training to encourage enthusiasm. Making progress increases a player's investment in the team, and with team success, they'll start believing in your tactics and training plan. Each year, the team added athletes who were passionate about the sport. The staff, Kevin Fickes, and I worked hard to develop the group as college players, and the athletes changed the program to one that expected success. Each season, expectations and standards rose. As the program began to change and we started finding regular success, a special instance occurred when a sophomore stepped up with a dream that changed how the program was thought of—and definitely changed his life.

"Hey Frank, I want to go pro," Tesho Akindele said to me.

Tesho began to do a special program for attacking players called Striker School, and soon, other players wanted to join in this directed practice. With that, our culture took a turn. We ramped everything up for him, and the other players brought new energy and excitement to our practices and matches. Tesho was influenced by a saying we had: "Winners Win." His character was a reflection of our culture, and our culture became a reflection of him. Everyone started going the extra mile and put in the work. That standard became a part of the Mines culture. Tesho went on to be a first-round pick and rookie of the year in Major League Soccer, in what became a successful nine-year career. His career was a testament to building culture and how it changes lives and teams.

Culture is the lifeblood of any successful team, organization, or business. Try to operate without one, and you may find fleeting success, but it will not be sustained. A strong culture starts with identifying each player's individual character and melding their traits together to establish a high standard that you want everyone to embody. In the early stages of culture development, when a player falls short, it's the staff who hold people accountable. As time passes and expectations are solidified, the team takes responsibility, reminding each other to Be All-In or Do It Now. In all of the schools I worked at, the student-athletes eventually became a pivotal part of maintaining the standard. And they didn't stop there; they went the extra mile without prompting.

That's how it was at USCS and UNC Charlotte. The guys wanted to play *all the time*—they couldn't get enough of soccer. That commitment brought them incredible success. Those additional practices helped them bond and work as a team. USCS's passion for competing at a high level led them to three Final Four runs. That culture extended to each season, qualifying the team for postseason every year except the first year of the program. It became a part of Charlotte's culture: to be fit, willing to defend, and always willing to compete. This is embodied by "Make It Happen," our second-season motto that led Charlotte to its first three NCAA Tournament appearances. It was a commitment to not wait around for progress or success to happen, but to intentionally make it happen.

As a group, determine your bare minimum, the lowest acceptable bar for staff and players alike. No matter the circumstances, everyone must function at or above that line—never below.

Culture Is Work

It's a running joke that when a coach (or strength trainer) looks away, it's the perfect opportunity for athletes to skip a set or half-ass a workout. Amusing in concept, but even this small decision is a telltale sign of an athlete's commitment, or lack of it, to the sport or workout.

There's a fitness exercise I include in most soccer training programs: Run 180 meters in 30 seconds, then take a one-minute rest before doing it again. On those occasions, when players stop short even one step, this is a shortcut—and not what a championship culture does. If people stop short, the whole team does it again. There are no excuses. Dropping below the standard is unacceptable; your opponent will not allow you to give less than your best if you want success. Everyone needs to meet the standard of the culture. It needs to become a habit to take every step and give it your all. Only then will it be ingrained in the culture to go all the way.

If you only do a training exercise one time, there's no clear answer on whether it'll work to produce the desired results. Repetition is when progress happens, both in sports training and in developing a culture. If an exercise doesn't work after sufficient time, that's when you switch it up. Some exercises become ingrained in your training program, a distinct part of the team. While you may adapt them year-to-year to suit your changing roster, you should have a training program that gets the team playing in a way that reflects your culture. Create a foundation that your team knows and can stick with. Your covenants come through in every training session you complete—as does your culture.

Know the Player

Of course, even with a well-ironed plan, there are going to be difficult players to bring into your culture. They will present problems every step of the way. As a coach, you have to decide if the fight is worth it. If not, maybe it's time for them to pack up their shit, turn in their gear, and not let the door hit them on their ass on the way out. On the flip side, some players are worth the fight. I had one guy (at least one in every program) who fought me at every turn, always saying, "Back where I'm from, we did it this way." He questioned most decisions or said what would be a better way for him—all of which interrupted our practices and caused us to have a strained relationship. Thankfully, I saw the potential in him. He needed more attention and direction. As a coach, your job isn't to provide equality; it's to make the experience fair (and equitable). Meet the players where they're at and address the individual needs. The player must be willing to meet the needs of the program as well. If there is no synchronicity, then neither the player nor the program will reach the highest possible level.

After communicating more with this player, we realized we were a lot alike, true competitors. Once we aligned and realized we weren't in competition with each other but with our opponents, he became a fabulous player. The staff had to show belief in him, and he showed he believed in the staff. He was worth fighting for, and the team was better because of it. (It will be interesting to see how many former athletes read this and wonder if they're that guy.) This is a classic example of man (player) management. When you know how to manage your players, you will get more out of your athletes. When the athlete is all-in, the experience is more rewarding for them, and their level reaches a new standard.

It can be daunting to align players of different backgrounds around one common goal. Take the time to get to know each of your athletes: their motivations, dreams, and goals. Pull out the best from each person, identifying player strengths and bringing those qualities into the culture. Use that information to define a goal of getting better every day. That has been the goal for every team I have coached, and also my personal goal. Make the main goal productive. Say you decide the goal is to be undefeated . . . and then you lose the first game. Team morale will drop, and the rest of the season may feel pointless. Don't set yourself up for failure. Instead, accompany the primary goal with your targets, such as winning a championship, allowing only one competitor goal per match, scoring two goals a match, etc. Stay true to making your athletes better and, therefore, your team better. Maintain the team's goal to improve as an athlete, person, and student every day, every way. Then, make a target that supports your overarching goal: to win against a specific competitor, make it to the NCAA tournament, etc. These targets lead to habits. The more your athletes embrace these winning habits, the better your culture will be, and the better your team and organization will be.

Final Thoughts

When assembling a staff, choose coaches with different experiences so that every person brings unique value to the team. There are veteran coaches who, like me, have decades of experience and have navigated every imaginable scenario. And then there are the younger, newer coaches who often speak the same language as the players and click differently with them. New coaches can even use their recent playing experience as a point of reference and relatability. The approach does not matter as long as the staff shares the same message on culture and standards. Once culture, standards, style of play, and training methods are decided, everyone must Be All-In and work together to be the team they are striving to become. Just like with the athletes, if a staff member is not all-in then they need to pack their shit.

As a coach, it would have been easy to place myself above the fray, act like I have a pass just for being in charge, but that's a novice oversight. I try to lead by example: eating healthy, staying in shape, and doing the exercise right alongside my players. I stay in the thick of it. The front of the bus has always been the unspoken assigned seating for administrators and coaches; it creates a distinct wall. So, I started sitting at the back of the bus, just to see what was going on and stay in tune with the team. It became a running joke: "When you're as old as I am, you have to be close to the bathroom." Regardless of where you choose to sit, you have to find ways to immerse yourself in the culture.

Start with some conversations *beyond* practices. Get to know them: where they come from, their aspirations, what drives them. Be willing to listen, both to your players and other coaches—you never know where you'll find inspiration. Establish rituals, like using songs to ramp up the energy and team spirit. With one team at Mines, we'd sing "Lean on Me." A little corny, but it was a way of saying we're all in. At Central Arkansas, the team would sing a victory song in the locker room, home or away, starting off quietly and then getting louder to boost our spirits and feel the joy. I can remember coaching the women's team at Mines. We'd sing the reggae song "Peace and Love" by Mishka on the bus after every win. After we lost in the Elite Eight, the captain came up to me and asked to play the song one last time. We may not have won the game, but we'd won the season—together.

These rituals and a cohesive mindset are what make a team. It's the culture you cultivate from day one that unites them, helping them play as one. After all, your team's success starts with the culture *you* create.

Philosophy Feeds Your Culture

To create a strong program, you need to ensure your philosophy and culture are bulletproof, ready to endure the wins and losses of a season. No matter how good a coach you are, there will be tough times, with setbacks alongside the successes. A philosophy provides the framework for your entire organization. It is the guiding basis and can be summarized in a few words: "No Regrets, No Excuses." "Pyramid of Joy."

I live by my Pyramid of Joy philosophy. When I broke my ankle, I went all-in for PT. The more I gave it my all, the sooner I could resume regular activities, placing me at the top of my Pyramid of Joy.

Building on philosophy is your culture—the covenants, core beliefs, and expectations of your program or organization. At UCA, we had those five defined, and when someone was lagging, we gave them a quick check, "#5, Do It Now." Culture starts with the individual character of the people involved, and it gives your program identity.

CHAPTER THREE

LEADERSHIP AND THE COACH–ATHLETE RELATIONSHIP

Early in my career, I encountered a leadership hurdle every coach eventually faces: playing with a man down. One of my USCS players was ejected from the game, and there was no one to sub in. I hadn't trained the team for this scenario, hadn't practiced for the unexpected. We lost the game 2–1.

In the locker room that day, I looked at the team and told them straight up, "We have to train for every situation." Then came a defining moment for me as a leader: "*I didn't prepare us to play a man down.*" I had to take accountability—that's the difference between a great leader and an average one. I wanted to be on a path to become a better leader. I may not have been on the pitch playing, but it was my oversight and lack of training that gave us the disadvantage—the team did the best they could with the skills they had. Shouldering a loss isn't easy, but as a leader, if you're responsible for everything, you have to be responsible for *everything*.

Following that fiasco, the staff and I made adjustments to the training plan and pushed the team hard, having them practice situationally with a player down and preparing for tough moments in a match. Ten matches down the road, our training paid off: We had two players sent off from the game. That could have been a sure loss, but instead, the team pulled together and won the match, 3–2. No one was surprised by our result, and I can say for certain that it was a testament to our hard work together in preparing for the tough, unexpected challenges that are possible in matches.

A coaching colleague of mine, Glenn Fisher, introduced me to a simple but powerful framework he uses with his swimmers called AIR: assess, interrupt, reframe. First, *assess* what went well and what didn't. For example, in the last match, we allowed a corner-kick goal because we didn't attack the ball in the air. We adjusted our training plan to address this weakness, learning to work on balls in the air. After you assess, *interrupt* the unproductive habits or behaviors. For us, we yelled "focus" whenever our opponents went for free kicks. Finally, we *reframed* to be more ready, changing our thinking and process to move forward more effectively. I've found this approach incredibly useful in my consulting work. When I sit down with a coaching staff, we start by identifying what worked well and what didn't. From there, we dig into areas that need improvement and work together to reframe the approach for better results.

Being a coach is more than a title and paycheck; it's leadership, accountability, and a drive to lead the team through the unknown.

Breathe, AIR

At Best Day Ever Consultancy, I suggest using this method for your team as you head into the last half or third of the season. By then, you should have a good idea of your current performance level versus where you want the team to be. This will help you see the path to success for a stronger finish to the season.

Assess the status of the team right now.

- What is working well?
- What is not working?
- What are the team's strengths? Weaknesses?

This is an evaluation of what has occurred with the team up until this point in the season. Gauging progress can be difficult—it requires a keen eye and honesty about where the team is, regardless of results. This is essential to becoming better.

Interrupt those areas that need to be improved. This follows your evaluation. If you're moving along the same path without any progress or positive results, then you have to accept that the approach isn't working. So the question becomes: What needs to change?

Leadership must consider all of the ways to pivot and remove the habits and practices that are considered counterproductive to the program's success or culture. Part of assessing to interrupt is to find the root of the good and bad. Consider how you can change the areas that need changing. How do you promote the positives you want to endure in the program?

Reframe your approach by deciding how the team is going to change to become better and how the program will be made better. The changes from your assessment will drive players and coaches to continue to improve their performances.

My friend, Glen Fisher, uses this in a different way to support individual athletes, but I liked the foundation and adapted it to work with teams.

Built on Character

Every person brings their distinct strengths to the team, and the staff is not exempt from this. Over time, my coaching persona has evolved into a stern but caring taskmaster, but it's up to each coach to define their role. By building leadership skills, you can organically take on a role that brings out the best in you and the team. A great leader is forged, meaning all types of coaching personalities can have a significant impact on their players—as long as they channel their passion and take the time to broaden their knowledge and skills.

One of the most important leadership skills is communication. You can't unify a team of diverse individuals around a singular goal *without* these interpersonal skills. If you know that's a weak point for you, make it an intentional area of growth—and Do It Now. Find a way to connect with your players and have those important conversations. These discussions could happen in the locker room after practice, on the bus as you travel to an away game, or even through a check-in chat during the off-season. Discuss where the program is at (the training plans, strengths, and areas to improve), where you're going (the goal and targets), and, most importantly, the *why* behind your decisions.

Some leaders, however skilled, forget to communicate the "why." Coaches face unpredictable situations on a regular basis; it's your job to pivot and find a solution. This could be a simple change during training or a significant lineup adjustment during the game—all are within your role as the coach. The mistake comes when you don't explain your reasoning to the players affected. That's when the drama starts, trust is broken, and feelings are hurt. A simple "I took you out because I want you fresh for the second half" can mitigate the situation before it gets out of hand. Without trust, nothing you say will resonate or stick with your team.

The learning curve for a new coach is immense, but passion helps you push through the challenges that come with the job. That passion can sometimes become so intense that it exacerbates a situation. One of the best tools I have is taking a breath to make a thought-out decision. It helps me respond appropriately rather than react emotionally, ensuring that my decision is intentional. That said, there are times when you take a breath and still choose to respond. I can remember a match years ago when I couldn't ignore a horrendous call against my team. I was very upset, and the opposing coach, Jeremy Gunn, saw it happen: "Frank, don't do it." He thought I was going to argue with the official, and even though it would have benefited him to have me fly off the handle, we had a respectful rivalry.

I winked at him, then told the referee what I thought of his delayed long-distance decision. I was tossed from the game . . . but this was all strategic. My removal was no big deal since I was already coaching the women's team in the next match. By standing up for our players, I showed the team I was all-in for them and would fight to make that clear. That's not to say that every call should be a fight. Few sports are as difficult to referee as soccer. As a young coach, I took opportunities to referee matches, so I would know what it takes to do the job. It was an area where I needed to develop my communication.

At the end of the day, your strongest leadership quality is caring about the people you coach—and showing them. Be vulnerable. Show them how you feel, and let them see the human behind the leader. As a young coach, I believed my actions went without saying, but to be effective, I learned they need to be verbalized. I showed up to practices, put in the work with each player, and gave the program my all. But I didn't *communicate* how much I cared to my players. Later in my career, I learned to try to voice how much being their coach meant to me. Athletes may not realize it in the moment, but in retrospect, they often say how much the journey meant to all of us involved.

I used to think that everyone should be treated the same. No favoritism, no special treatment. Now, with decades of experience, I know that everyone should be treated *fairly*. It's the difference between equality (giving everyone the same opportunities) and equity (leveling the playing field). By addressing the individual needs of your team, you're positioned to make the most of their skills. People bring different levels of all-in to the program. Those who are all-in need to know you recognize their commitment. Gifted and committed athletes will have the highest expectations in training, in matches, and off the field. Many coaches allow their best players to slide when these players deserve to be pushed to reach their ceiling. This allows your team to be better, and just like the Tesho example earlier, it pushes the entire program because the best is being asked to do their best.

Coaching is not one playbook for success; take it from someone who has followed an unconventional path. Unlike many other coaches, I spent my teenage and young adult years playing all kinds of sports and learning game management and strategies that carry over regardless of sport. I did not always get to play organized soccer, which could have put me at a disadvantage, but I took these as opportunities to learn, seek advice from others, and define my approach to coaching. Faced with so many unpredictable situations, I learned to use these experiences to help me grow. Be confident in your skills, yes, but be willing to learn from your fellow coaches. See the opportunities along with the pitfalls. Face mistakes with some humor and accountability. You don't walk into this job knowing how to handle every moment—you learn from the grind, through mistakes, and through the moments that test you. With time, you will learn how to connect with your team, how to earn respect, and how to keep growing, no matter how long you've been in the game.

Lead from the Center

The best teams and organizations include people from different backgrounds. This provides a breadth of knowledge and experiences to pull from, but it can also feel disjointed. As a coach, it's your job to pull individuals together to make a successful team. Part of this unity comes from understanding each other. Take the time to get to know each person on your team. Soccer gives you a place to start, but move the conversation further. Understand their season goals, long-term dreams, and even how they see themselves. More often than not, people will need a dose of reality or motivation to reach higher. Help them overcome that doubt and see the possibilities, not their version of reality. Facilitate team-building moments and go beyond the regular icebreaker of name, major, and graduation date. Some of our best bonding sessions were chats following practice or took place over food, often cooked at the Soccer House by one of our players. Many were unprompted, but by making myself available, we were able to have those valuable exchanges and strengthen the coach-athlete relationship. Those are the moments that unify a team. Some of the moments that bond your team the most are when extraordinary situations occur in the program or to a teammate. This is the way life happens, and whether it is shared moments of celebration like an underdog victory or joining together to relieve sorrow, as the team did when one of our player's parents passed away, it's in these moments that you realize how connected you are. The whole team rallied around that player. These formative moments are when the extended family of the team can make such a difference for all involved. These are also the times when the team realizes that they mean more to you than their stats!

Three years ago, we had a Muslim player, Karim Diao, who observed Ramadan. As it requires an all-day (sunrise to sunset) fast for 29–30 days, the effect on the team was inescapable. Rather than viewing it as a problem, I turned it into a teachable moment. The player told the team all about the holiday, and some of the players fasted for a day just to see what he was going through. I joined as well, fasting for a week to see the world through his perspective. It was incredible and reminded the team to find appreciation in life and empathy for others. The experience brought the team closer together. Timing practice around the breaking of his fast wasn't viewed as an inconvenience—it became a celebration and talking point. Recruiting brings talent from all corners of the world. As a leader, you must explore the differences, find common ground, and fortify those player relationships— this is critical for success, both on the pitch and as a team. By taking the time to know and understand each other, we maximize our potential. After all, training will only get you so far.

Turning Players into Leaders

As a coach, you can't be everywhere at once. That's why you need an ironclad culture that defines the team's standard so your players can lead their teammates. I start a player's leadership journey early, taking an exceptional freshman or sophomore and pairing them with an upperclassman who embodies our culture. This mentor isn't always the big star on the team who has the most talent; instead, I look for someone who lives by example, just as the coaches do. The strongest teams have leadership from the staff, from the team, and from the athletes.

The responsibilities start small—"plan a team meal"—then become more serious—"lead your group in the training session today." It's crucial that if you establish a leader for the team, you put your trust in them. Offer support and encourage their decisions; the results won't always be favorable, but that's when you AIR.

Whether someone is a team captain or simply a strong team leader, ensure the messaging is the same and the standards remain high. When players lead, your team becomes a force of autonomy, capable of making split-second decisions on the pitch. And on training days, they hold each other accountable, maximizing their combined potential. Good players can turn into good leaders—as a coach, you need to spot them early and empower them to win. When you have leaders from within the team, it strengthens your culture and makes your program better.

CHAPTER FOUR

THE MAVERICK METHOD

When people think of Tom Cruise as Maverick in *Top Gun*, they picture a reckless daredevil who puts aside the safety of others. A guy who ignores orders, follows his gut, and somehow still ends up on top. What they often overlook is that Maverick isn't solely creating chaos—he's taking chances in ways most people are too afraid to try. At UNC Charlotte, we had an athlete who looked so much like Cruise that we nicknamed him Mav, and he was often stopped in airports to sign autographs. His teammates did not mind being his (Darren Feeney) wingman. Maverick refuses to play it safe or stick to the status quo because he believes in something better, something more efficient. You don't have to risk your life by any means, but this kind of progress and success comes when you learn from everyone, copy no one, and are bold enough to step outside your comfort zone.

My mindset has been shaped by years of watching, listening, and coaching. I didn't care if it was someone's first day or their twentieth year; I wanted to see how they taught, what worked, and how I might adapt it to my own coaching abilities. Every coach I've ever encountered has left a mark on me: Some inspired me to learn from their lessons, while others taught me what would not work for me. I've joked with my players, "If you can't be anything else, be a bad example." Oddly enough, that's some of the best advice I've ever followed. There's value in every experience, good or bad. Look to borrow ideas, tweak strategies, and make a drill your own—just ensure you don't try to copy someone else's exactly; that type of shortcut won't bring results. Every team that has been successful, from your local team to the World Cup, has a way of playing that is uniquely theirs. I can remember talking with a top-level, highly respected coach who was worried about someone copying his plan. I said to him, "Jeremy, don't worry. No one can present the plan to their team like you can." People may try to imitate him, but coaches who learned from his abilities and adapted them to their strategies saw the best results.

My coaching path has always been different; I've coached all sorts of sports with different team sizes around the country, so I never worried about someone taking my style. When Robbie Church, who recently retired as Duke University's head women's soccer coach, and I watched his son coach for Michigan basketball, we talked about their tactics and walked away with ideas we could carry over to our coaching perspectives. That kind of crossover thinking? That's a Maverick move.

You can pull tactics from all sports, but basketball is where I see the strongest synergy. In defending, whether it's soccer or basketball, the better you move from man-to-man to zone to match-up zone, the more you throw off your opponent. There are times to put a body on a body or to help out a teammate with a screen (basketball) or takeover (soccer). The positioning and movements are similar, and at the end of the day, it's all about the same principle: Deny the other team a clear path to the goal. Same strategy, just adapted to a different sport. When your team starts to take pride in the grind, that's when underdogs become dawgs—a current term for those athletes who embrace the grind and the grit that others will not work toward. Once you become a dawg, you can move on to become a winner, and then a champion, and then continue to build the program by elevating others to your level.

From Underdogs to Topdogs

The underdog mentality has been deeply rooted in sports. Stories like "US shocks England in 1950 World Cup" and the 1980 US Olympic men's ice hockey team, more famously known as "Miracle on Ice," prove there's nothing more powerful than beating the odds.[1] But it wasn't luck that had them walk away as victors—it was discipline. They trained harder, fought longer, and did the work others avoided because it seemed "too difficult." The upset is the beauty of sport and starts with the belief in doing the work that the favored team did not find necessary. From the first drill after warm-ups to packing up your gear in the locker room after practice, everything should be intentional. We're not just running practice, we're building habits and shaping a mindset. One of my favorite training setups is small-sided games—three versus three with a goalkeeper. The format tells you everything you need to know about a player because there's no hiding in a 3v3.

[1] "USA Shock England in 1950: The Miracle on Grass," posted November 15, 2012, by FIFA, YouTube, 5 min., 45 sec., https://www.youtube.com/watch?v=U4ESTvxyqsl.

This reveals if they are a complete player. Everyone has to attack, defend, recover, press, and compete. And if you don't? It shows.

As coaches, we're there driving the standard and motivating the players, but it's ultimately up to the players to break out of the mold and shine. Their results are a big part of their progress feedback. Only they can decide if they're content being an underdog. In those moments of self-discovery, players reveal themselves—not just by how they play, but by how they respond to the pressure of being accountable to their teammates and themselves. Can they take that pressure and transform it into motivation to become the best athlete, or do they break under scrutiny? During these small-sided games, we'll match our top three midfielders against the next three and so on. Interestingly, small-sided teams with defenders almost always win in these drills because those defenders enjoy what other positional players may look at as suffering and work. When your team is making real progress, they are moving to the top of the Pyramid of Joy, enjoying the hard work, becoming more fit, and competing at a high standard every opportunity. You could throw together your most gifted attackers, and more often than not, they'll struggle because defense is about structure and accountability; it's about being a complete player, and for some reason, only the rare attacker has added this to their repertoire (we coaches have allowed this and, in many cases, still allow it). And that's what you have to instill in every player: the drive to be the complete player.

We'll mix up the lines and place players in unfamiliar roles to help them grow more comfortable under pressure. A Maverick approach requires this ability to pivot. Remember in the last chapter when we had to play a man down without a plan? Don't set yourself or your players up to fail. Instead, train them to adapt by preparing them for the unexpected, and ensure they're ready for whatever the game throws their way.

That's my goal every day as a coach. Not just turning players into better athletes, but turning them into better people by pushing them to be accountable, resilient, and ready for more than just match day. Because when they leave your program, it shouldn't just be with sharper foot skills or a better shot—it should be with a stronger sense of self. Respect and kindness change the world!

Finding Your Balance

Once you instill that competitive fire, the next challenge is finding the balance between conditioning, technical drills, mental toughness, and tactical drills. You can run a team into the ground with conditioning training, but what if they can't connect two passes, follow a plan, or read the game?

The best training exercises are the ones that hit all areas at once. You get more out of your players when they're not just running for the sake of running. The work should mean something. People used to say, "Frank's teams just run." There's some truth to it. We did lots of training exercises that included a running component because it's not bowling, it's soccer. A midfielder might cover 15k in a game, but I made sure the team also played, competed, and executed at the same time. And most of the time, we accomplished it all in one training exercise.

Sometimes you have to isolate a technical piece like clearing the ball in the defensive third or playing in two touches under pressure in the midfield. Or maybe it's finishing, and you want to give your attackers reps that feel real. I remember one time coaching with Real Colorado, a top-level youth club, and this young coach told me, "Hey Frank, if you need the goals, go ahead, I won't be using them today."

Confused, I asked, "So you're not working on finishing?"

"Well, finishing's only one percent of the game."

I thought, *Well, it's actually 100 percent of winning a match.* "I'll take the goals because we're interested in getting better at that one percent thing." It's a coach's job to ensure the team is always getting better at the most difficult part of the sport.

Finishing isn't the only skill that matters, but it's a pretty crucial part of the game—one that I can't believe many coaches don't focus on at every training. While it's important to develop certain skills, there are crucial factors to every game, such as finishing, that require consistent work. That's why I always encourage a holistic approach to coaching, because it delivers the best results.

Whenever we could, my staff and I tried to blend the elements of the sport. Physical, technical, mental, and tactical. A lot of American teams get caught up in the possession game, but soccer isn't all about passing. It's also about reading the field and finding the gaps—skills that are critical to practice. At the end of the day, soccer, at its core, is simple. We complicate it too much, but the game itself is beautiful in its simplicity. Score goals and don't allow goals—it's the beautiful game for a reason!

Mental Toughness and Mental Health _____

Mental toughness has become a critical focus in sports, especially considering the amount of pressure student-athletes face today. We addressed this by bringing in a sports psychologist, Dr. Dan Freigang, to work directly with our UCA and Mines teams, and we encouraged our athletes to take advantage of the school counselors, which really helped create a more supportive environment. Thankfully, awareness around mental health has come a long way. There's still a stigma, but the conversation is opening up and continuing to play a big part in how we train our athletes.

As coaches, we're not always part of an athlete's mental health journey unless they choose to involve us. Still, we're often among the first to notice when something doesn't seem right. A sudden dip in performance, a change in body language, or a shift in how they interact with teammates. Maybe they stop making eye contact, seem quieter, or are a bit more irritable than usual. It's subtle, but noticeable if you're paying attention. That's why it's important, as a coach, to make a habit of checking in with each other. Simple things like, "Did you notice how he seemed today?" or "Something felt off with him during training." It's not about trying to fix the situation; it's about showing up, being present, and giving the players a support system they can count on. Sometimes, just knowing someone is paying attention can be a turning point for a young athlete.

Freshmen, especially, tend to carry the brunt of the stress. New school, new teammates, and collegiate-level expectations can be a lot to handle. Freshmen are trying to find their place while also proving they belong. That intimidation factor is real. But as long as it doesn't cross into serious mental health concerns, a little discomfort can actually be a positive. Growth doesn't happen in comfort zones. With a growth mindset, that discomfort becomes an opportunity to get better, stronger, and sharper. Our job as coaches is to guide them through that process and help them find a new level while keeping our expectations known. We assess everything: their skill level, mindset, maturity, and how they compare to returning players. That evaluation starts immediately and shapes how we coach each athlete. But it's not just about calling out mistakes. With younger players, especially, it's important to highlight what they're doing well to build that trust and comfort level between player and coach. Once that foundation is there, then you can challenge them to reach higher.

On the other end of the spectrum, your most talented players should never be the ones getting a free pass. Too often, coaches let them slide by if they show up late, wear whatever they want, skip reps, or whatever it may be, only because they're the star player. This sends the wrong message to the team. Your best players should be held to the highest standards. This helps them reach a new standard, and they set the tone for everyone else. The longer you have been around in the program, the better you should reflect the standards and culture of the program.

Freshmen should be looking up to those players not because they're flashy or high-scoring, but because they show up on time, give a hand up, lead by example, and show what coachable looks like. That's the kind of culture and intention that builds real, lasting success.

The Holy Grail of Training Techniques

One of the biggest game-changers in modern-day coaching is film. When I first started out, we had reel-to-reel, cut and splice, but now advanced technology is everywhere and offers incredible value. Film gives athletes clarity. You may not see a Maverick bloom on-screen, but you *can* play back the footage to show mistakes or celebrate corrections, strengthening player capabilities and confidence.

As a coach, you can say, "Right there—that's exactly what we want." Even if they only nailed it once, that one clip becomes a reference point for the athlete. On the flip side, you can show what didn't work, why it didn't, and how a different approach makes more sense. Beyond your own footage, there's also an endless stream of high-level play available from services like TV, YouTube, and most streaming platforms. Watching what professionals do in the same scenarios can be incredibly powerful for fellow athletes.

But video footage is only part of it. Another crucial piece is imitating real-game scenarios in training. The intensity and tempo of your training sessions should mirror the conditions of match day as closely as possible so your athletes are prepared. That means building competitiveness into everything, from warm-ups to tactical drills. Sometimes that means modifying numbers. If your starting 11 is facing a high-pressure team, you might have them play against 13 in training. Why? Because it simulates a tighter time and space, forcing faster decision-making and better communication amongst teammates. By challenging them, you build familiarity with the possible chaos and pace they'll face on game day.

Every training session should reflect your match model. Whether it's a 1v1, a 3v3, or a full 11v11 scenario, it should serve a purpose. You're not just filling time with practices; you're preparing them to properly execute when it matters. No matter the focus of the day, I ended every practice with the team playing. The love of the game comes from playing. Let them go at it so they can feel the game, enjoy it, push each other, and compete. It doesn't mean throwing structure out the window. You can create match-like conditions: 10 minutes down a goal or 10 minutes with a player down. But end the training session with the reason why they chose to be an athlete. Let the players play. Players who wholeheartedly love playing soccer will move up the Pyramid of Joy during this time.

Having a weekly training plan is essential, but the successful coaches know how to adapt on the fly. The best teams have a Plan A and a Plan B, but the really good ones have a Plan C too. Just like in a match, not everything in training will go exactly to plan. A session might not click right away, and that's okay. Don't toss it out just because the first run-through fell flat. Maybe the players didn't understand what you were trying to get at, or maybe the timing or setup was off. So you adjust, revisit it later, and give it a fair shot. That said, sometimes things click, and when they do, you need the flexibility to run with it. If you're in the middle of a training week and you hit on something where suddenly everything aligns—the players get it, the energy is high, the execution is sharp— you lean in to what that session can provide. You might've only budgeted 15 minutes for the training exercise in your plan, but if it's working, let it run. Revisit it the next day and see what happens.

Any time we lost a match, we switched up our uniform for the next one, even if it was just a change of socks. But if we won a match, we would wear the exact same uniforms. It might seem like superstition, but to me, there's a lesson: If something's not working, don't repeat it. This shows up outside of sports all the time. People leave a bad relationship or job only to end up in the same situation again. Comfort can be blind, but true growth requires reflection—asking what worked, what didn't, and then making a change. So, whether it's coaching or life, the takeaway is simple: Play to your strengths, minimize your weaknesses, and don't be afraid to pivot. It's not superstition—it's strategy. If it works, keep rolling back out there. If it doesn't work, find a way to change it to make your team better!

Planning around load and recovery is also huge. Work backward from your match day, so if the game is on Saturday, then everything in your plan is built to peak for that. Most coaches now refer to it in matchday terms— matchday minus one and so on. It might sound a little dramatic, like you're prepping for a space launch, but it actually helps structure the week with purpose. It gives an edge for the athletes to feel the intensity.

Be a Maverick

Coaching isn't about everything going perfectly, it's about responding when it doesn't. That fractured ankle five minutes into a session? It can happen. You have to pivot and get creative. You have to model resilience to build it into your training culture. These are the moments that require you to know the difference between being nice versus showing kindness. Being nice is always saying something nice, no matter what, whereas being kind, you tell your athletes the truth because you care for them and want them to grow and develop. I used to say, "My mom named me Frank for a reason." Using 3v3 and film are the best times to be a truth teller and use your kindness to help your athletes get better every day.

More than anything else, your training plan has to push players out of their comfort zone. I used to talk to fellow coaches all the time about how players come in with these boxes in their heads that they put themselves in. Limitations or expectations from old coaches or influenced by something they saw Lionel Messi or Barca do on TV. We'd go to the whiteboard, draw a box labeled comfort zone, and way out in the corner, draw a big X and say: "You know what that is? That's where the good shit is." Every day in training, our goal was to help them move beyond the expected, to chase that X and step outside of their box. Mav was once involved in one of these moments as we were headed to a spring match against the University of North Carolina and had no healthy fullbacks.

He was normally a forward, but he was pivotal in helping us win that exhibition match. From then on, Mav became a stalwart defender; he became an example of helping our athletes become more complete players who were willing to reach for that X.

The Bold Path Forward

The original mavericks were cows that had never been branded or gathered. They knew the best trails to get food, water, and shade. Sometimes, the herd would catch on and begin to follow the path of the maverick cattle. I've followed an untraditional coaching path, finding the best opportunities and experiences. As a maverick, you learn from everyone, copy no one, and are bold enough to step outside your comfort zone.

CHAPTER FIVE

THE TRAIL TO BEING A BETTER COACH

Nothing about my career has been conventional. Growing up in a military family meant we were constantly on the move, so most of the sports I played were pickup games with the other Air Force kids—unstructured competition or base leagues, all with a love of the game. Even my college years weren't much different. Most coaches work their way through the ranks: volunteer work, youth leagues, club teams, then assistant coaching, all leading up to their big break as head coach. No surprise that I skipped a few steps, working as a head coach for 17 years before I ever took an assistant coach role. In the break between my job at UNC Charlotte, the Raleigh Flyers, and the Richmond Kickers, I volunteered to be an assistant coach for Davidson College alongside their head coach, Charlie Slagle, who was a longtime rival and friend.

It was a different world of coaching. For the first time, I wasn't setting the tone or playing the disciplinarian who dealt out consequences. I locked in, not just to the strategy but to a new side of the players. The relationship became uncomplicated: I could zero in on specific players to develop and find ways to elevate their skills—all in an effort to perform as I would have wanted an assistant to work together with me. I supported the head coach and pushed the players to be better each day. Each part of the staff contributes something to the leadership team; as an assistant coach, I learned to be an active participant by adding to the training. Although an unexpected detour, this experience taught me what to look for and expect from my assistant coaches. Success in coaching doesn't come from a set path—it's about showing up, growing, and learning to lead in every opportunity you encounter.

Whatever your ideal path, look for examples of coaches who are where you want to be. See what makes them successful and what formative experiences helped them get to that point. You can have your idols, but not every successful coach will be a good example for the career path you want to follow. Case in point: If you're not a taskmaster who can stay on top of things, it wouldn't do to totally follow my approach as a head coach, but there are areas to learn from and make your own. There are many areas to learn from, so shape those ideas to fit your coaching personality. Start networking, and most importantly, watching how other coaches work. To reach the top, you must be willing to study from the best by observing what sets them apart, learning from their strengths, and applying those lessons to your journey. Don't be fooled by who wins trophies; many times, the leader doing the best job is the one getting the most out of a group with less talent and fewer resources. Keep honing your craft, and in time, your distinct approach will come into its own.

As you start to define your ideal job and career path, take a beat to AIR your skills: *Assess* your current skills and the areas for growth, *interrupt* any bad behaviors or habits, and *reframe* to improve, developing skills to become better than you were before. Learn to AIR on a regular basis, especially as you gain experience. At the start of my career, I focused on listening and learning from fellow and veteran coaches. When I attended conferences, I rarely spoke up—except to ask questions and learn. Many new coaches try to prove themselves and overcompensate with tales of their knowledge. They end up thinking so much about what they are going to say next and end up not listening. That's not to say you should mentally check out once your career hits a certain number of years. Continue to listen to your coaching staff, to other leaders, and the people you admire. You always learn more from listening than from talking. You're never too experienced to gain more knowledge.

Now, as an older and more seasoned coach, I'm asked to tell stories and share my hard-earned knowledge. One of the biggest pieces of advice I can give is to stay away from trends. You must remain strong to do what is best for your program, regardless of what the latest popular way to play is. You can switch up drills, but make sure you are finding *your* best way, not what's popular. An effective coach is one who offers consistency with adaptability. The minute you try to play like everyone else, you're at a disadvantage. Let's face it: You won't beat them at their game—you have to fight yours. One of the best approaches I ever implemented didn't come from a book or another team: It was pure Maverick. At UNC Charlotte, we played a season with three backs, three defensive midfielders, three attacking midfielders, a striker, and a goalkeeper. We only had one striker and a group of good midfielders, so it was necessary to come up with a plan that would work for us. It worked great for us and often left our competitors asking, "What the hell system are they playing?" Automatic advantage. Continue studying the game, and you'll identify your advantage. Consider: How do I get my best group out there doing what suits them best? Make the most of the ingredients you have. In this case, we had a lot of talented mids and only one striker. We used this system again years later when I coached the Colorado ODP with Marcelo Balboa, and we managed to win a national championship. You don't need Shakespearean complexity—just authenticity.

With every coach taking a different path to success, with varying peaks and trails to navigate, there's no prescribed "end." Define what success looks like to you and make every decision a step toward that goal. Some coaches achieve an incredible win and then lose motivation. To overcome this stagnant mindset, you need to identify a new challenge and take it up to the next level. Wins and losses won't sustain you for long; I encourage you to instead look at the effect you have on others and the impact it can have on your life.

My wife, Deb, is the perfect example of what it means to be all-in. She is an amazing example of how, if you care for someone, you must care for their passion. I could not have chosen a better partner to support me through my winding coaching career. At every signpost along the trail, she became ingrained in our team culture. Some coaches make the mistake of keeping their work and home lives separate, but I suggest the opposite. To this day, when I talk to former Spartanburg players, the first question they ask is "Hey, how's Deb doing?" It reflects just how deeply she became part of their lives. Deb has a favorite team in the PL and even participates in fantasy leagues with former players! My coaching trail wouldn't be complete without her—it never has been. A key point to enjoying and enhancing this journey is having someone to share it with.

Cut? Keep Climbing

Coaching, particularly at the collegiate level, is known for its high turnover rate. No matter how hard you work, some paths simply don't work out. You may get fired or not be offered a new contract, or there are times when the program is downsized or cut entirely. These elements are out of your control; what you *can* control is how you react. Take the time for that first reaction of anger or sadness, but then use the emotion as inspiration. You grow when you face your hardest challenges. Those unexpected job changes showed me just how much being a coach meant. It wasn't a job to earn a paycheck—it was my passion. Losing that, even briefly, made me a better person. I had more appreciation for the top of the Pyramid of Joy once I found a new program and athletes to work with. A job lost or unrenewed contract is never easy, but let that become a motivator to push harder. Every challenge is a marker on your coaching trail.

You can fight, flee, or go with the flow. At every turn, I'm fighting. I will always fight for my team, as I consider them an extension of my family. You have to be willing to put your team first and make sure they have the best possible experience in your program. At times, that might mean you step on some toes. I can remember being in a job interview where I was faced with an unwavering loyalty to the school or holding strong to my values and principles.

I thought to myself, *This has to be a trick question . . . who would ask someone to forgo their life principles?* Up to that point—and to this day—I've been proud of the legacy I've built with my teams. I will always stay true to my principles and continue to fight for my kids, as should you.

When you lose a match, you don't give up. You look back at what you could've done differently and apply it to the next match. The same goes for when you lose a job. You can't sit around, hoping a job lands in your lap. It's during those lows on your trail where you find yourself improving because that's your only option.

You may go through the turmoil of, *Now I don't have a job. Will we have to sell the house? Get food stamps?* Here's the best part: You didn't have a job when you got your first job. Although losing a job changes your trail and adds more valleys and pinnacles to get to the top of the mountain, the joy you will feel reaching the top will make it worthwhile. Use this valley as your fire to become a better coach. I'm the first to say I'm not a perfect coach. There are many who enjoyed our time together and a few who did not. But I made sure to try my damn best every day for my team. This is the key to knowing you are all-in to build that program and help those in it grow.

The Final Stop

When I look back at my coaching career, I want my former athletes to be at the forefront. The effect that you have on athletes is often underestimated; you're not just affecting them during the time they play for you, you're impacting the way they grow up, the way they see themselves, how they raise their kids, and so much more. I recently had surgery to repair a broken ankle, and I received a number of texts, calls, and emails from past athletes who wanted to check on me—some just to say, "Let's run those trails," or "180s now!"

Moments like those are when I say to myself, *Yeah, it has been a wonderful journey—with more trails to travel and sights still to see.*

The impact you make on your athletes stays with them for years. I see them having families and successful businesses and following their own trail, whether it's on a highway or the road less traveled. It's my job to show them all the options, all the roads that they can take, but after that, they'll need to become their own tour guide to the Pyramid of Joy.

Aligning Passion with Purpose

Reflect on where you want to go: Do you want to offer support through an assistant coach position? Perhaps you have a specific area of focus that you excel at, making you perfect for specialized coaching (strength, goalkeeping, special teams, set plays, etc.). Or maybe you prefer to call the plays or create a training program as head coach. If head coach is the path for you, be prepared to wake up every day with the mission to make improvements to yourself and your team. Regardless of the title and prestige, the best role for you is subjective. Consider: What are the areas and skills you can control to reach your dream? Find opportunities that can become a stepping stone to your end goal.

NO REGRETS, NO EXCUSES

While coaching USCS, we had an away match in St. Augustine, Florida, right after a hurricane hit there. The team and I stepped onto the pitch and saw several inches of water sloshing on the grass. Without a second thought, the guys accepted the conditions and got warm-ups underway. They jogged across the pitch and turned back toward the touchline, suddenly breaking into a full sprint. Together, they jumped headfirst into a slide through the water, as suggested by their leaders, Martin Hill, Roger Watt, and Paul McGinty. Other teams may have gotten in their heads, accepted the slippery pitch as a loss they couldn't prevent, but these guys weren't going to let a few inches of rain bother them—in fact, it seemed to fuel their win. Fast forward to when I coached the women's soccer team at Mines, and a similar circumstance happened. All four seasons of weather came down on us ahead of an NCAA Tournament match at Fort Lewis, and I had previously told the team about the challenging conditions for the St. Augustine match. The girls lined up for their warm-ups, and next thing I knew, they were all sliding in the mud and snow with big, bright smiles. The team embraced the conditions and pulled off a spectacular win.

After they were done, the captain, Pocket Rocket, came up to me and said, "Now you can tell stories about us." Here I am, telling that story—one of unrelenting teams who made the best of each day.

In the face of the unexpected, I taught the athletes I trained to find a way through challenges they will inevitably face. As a coach, your entire job is pivoting to navigate the unknown, whether that be competing with an athlete down for the first time, losing a job, or unexpectedly playing with several inches of rain on the pitch. There's a former athlete I coached at UNC Charlotte who recently opened another restaurant with his twin brother, Carlos, and Gabe Garcia, following success with their Mexican cuisine restaurants, El Chapparel. This time, they opened a burger place (Twin Bros Burgers) in San Antonio, Texas. Their new restaurant's motto? Make It Happen! The motto is one of those from our days together. It's an important mindset and not limited to my athletes; I hold myself up to this standard as well. Even when I parted ways with a school or organization, I didn't let that get me down. Instead, it motivated me to get back up, to remember who I am and what I can bring to the next organization.

Even now, walking dogs for the animal shelter or doing PT to help post-ankle surgery, I give it my all. When I'm at the shelter, I give 100 percent to those dogs. They deserve my attention and commitment for each mile we walk together. Same with my ankle recovery. I strategically balance resting with physical activity because that's when the true progress happens. Each day is a conscious effort to give 100 percent of myself to improve. Life, particularly as a coach, isn't a straightforward path to get to the peak. You don't need a trail map to start the journey—just give each step your all. Take your next step every day!

In decades of coaching, I gave each team my best. Coaches hold an incredible amount of power to influence hundreds of lives, and I've always taken the position seriously, acting with full intention and determined effort. Looking back at the competitors I've faced since entering the coaching profession, I realize how lucky I've been to be immersed in my passion, which has encouraged and uplifted me during those times. Without those people in my life, I surely would have stumbled more on my trail working toward the Best Day Ever.

That's the core lesson from my years in soccer and the foundation of my consulting business, Best Day Ever Soccer Consulting and Coaching for teams and leaders of organizations. I started the business by happenstance. While involved in a match, I noticed a younger yet high-potential soccer coach struggling with a result his team encountered despite their evident skills. I started to chat with him, listened to his struggles, and offered guidance for improvement. With that reassurance, I said goodbye and didn't think about it again . . . until a few months later, after we were both encouraged by our friend, Dr. Dano, and I received a call from the coach asking if I would be interested in becoming a consultant for his team. We put in the work together, pursued results, and have become good friends since.

I didn't start a consulting business for recognition or praise—the driving motivation has been my desire to help other leaders, coaches, programs, and schools achieve their Best Day Ever every day by putting in the work to propel their organization. The success will come when you follow the trail that works best for your group. Enter each day with an open mind to the potential it offers.

I find myself walking into restaurants, doctors' offices—you name it—and analyzing the way things are run. *What's the best way for them to be most effective? Which of their people are all-in for their program?* That's how I approach each client. I also hit them with the *why*— the most important part of every endeavor. Just like I did with the athletes I worked with to find success. I'll tell an athlete that they won't start, instead playing later to come in fresh. But I don't stop there; I explain *why I made that choice.* This was a change I needed to make from my days as a young coach, thinking the athletes would know and understand each decision without me communicating it. Without explaining yourself and your thought process, you'll have a tough time trying to get your players to understand. Show them you care and put thought into each decision. The transparency will make it easier for people to buy into what you're saying. In order for the Best Day Ever to happen, there needs to be a defined plan, with 100 percent commitment.

At the end of the day, it's not about being in the spotlight—it's about helping others shine by leading with purpose, clarity, and most importantly, heart.

It's my love of soccer and my passion for coaching athletes that have most defined my "legacy." I'm proud to see my athletes making a life for themselves, inspiring those around them, and always striving for greatness. As for me, I'll continue Best Day Ever Consulting in order to help as many people as possible achieve their Best Day Ever, fill my days with volunteering at the animal shelter, and spend some well-deserved time with Deb. The position of "the coach's partner" can be a lonely one, and not a day goes by that I'm not appreciative of the sacrifices she has made for my goals and dreams. I wouldn't be the coach or man I am today without Deb, and for that, I owe her everything.

My career has never really been about the wins or losses. Although it's fun to know that the teams I worked with made it to 40 post-seasons as a group, leading to moments of joy and celebration—it's always been about the people. The players, coaches, friends, family. It's about the lessons we carry off the competition fields and into our lives: intention, purpose, empathy, and reflection. I've always believed in showing up fully, giving my best, and helping others do the same. Whether it was navigating a career shift or helping a coach with potential find his footing, my goal has always been to make a difference one Best Day at a time. I'm grateful for every step of this adventure through my Pyramid of Joy, for those who walked beside me, and for the opportunity to keep moving down my unconventional path.

TIPS FROM GREAT COACHES TO BUSINESS AND ORGANIZATION LEADERS

I've had the privilege of working alongside some incredible coaches in my career. With each opportunity, I sat back and listened, ready to pick up wisdom to apply to my approach. Below are some of the best practices I've gathered. Remember, learn from everyone, copy no one, and be bold enough to step outside your comfort zone.

- **Show Up with a Smile**

  Every day you come into work, show your team that you are excited to be there and passionate about the work! The best leaders show up every day like there is nowhere else they would rather be. If you want your team to be enthusiastic about the work, you have to set the example.

  For business leaders, the people you guide will mirror the energy you bring into the workplace. Show up with a smile because, as a leader, you want to be there facing the day with your team. If you want your workers to have a positive approach, it starts with your positivity.

- **Set High Standards and Lay Out a Road Map**

  If you want your team to achieve great accomplishments, goals, and targets, then the expectations and standards must not only be high, but also be clear. As their leader, you must embody these standards. Give your team the needed equipment and training, both physically and mentally, to reach the necessary levels to accomplish your set goals and targets.

  These standards are more meaningful when leaders encourage team members to be a part of setting the standards and determining the plan for success. Teams, companies, and organizations achieve great only when greatness is asked of them. So ask your team the questions, but give them the material to find the answers that work!

- **Take Stock of What Your Team Has and Build on the Positive**

  Don't waste time or energy on what your team lacks or what your competitors have. Great leaders concentrate on how to make the most of the people and ingredients that are part of their program. Coaches and leaders are always trying to improve the situation by training and enhancing their people and equipment.

  Top managers guide their team to make the most of what they have and face challenges together. Your group makes progress when the team optimizes its components. It's a waste to spend energy thinking about what another team, business, or organization has working for them. Get your team in the mindset of "the best us!"

- **Be Simple, Efficient, and Accountable**

  When bringing new ideas or personnel into your group, make the explanation *simple* so the role of the changes is easily understood. The change should make the operation and your approach to a goal more *efficient*, improving the path to what you are striving to achieve. Finally, hold the improvements *accountable* in order to see if the new ideas and new people have improved the team. SEA makes each team better.

- **Get Better Every Day**

  Whether your group is coming off a championship or stuck in a losing streak, you must strive to be better than you were yesterday. "If it ain't broke, don't fix it" is not a good line if you are striving to reach your ceiling. While you may be satisfied where you are, your competition is changing to catch up and pass you.

- **Build Freedom and Creativity Through Discipline**

  Great leaders build discipline into every individual in the program. Having consistency from everyone in effort, focus, and understanding leads to creativity and freedom. The basics are taken care of through the team's discipline.

- **Find an Advisor, Mentor, or Truthteller**

  The best leaders have someone in their inner circle who helps them stay on track toward the target. In order to improve, you need an advisor or consultant—ask their advice and learn from their experiences. This can make a significant difference in achievement.

Have a thinking partner you can believe in and who believes in you!

- **Show Your Appreciation**

  Take time to show your appreciation for everyone involved in helping the program succeed. Whether it is the smallest job or an essential task, great leaders are thankful and mindful that everyone makes a difference and improves the entire program. By rewarding hard work with appreciation, individuals will keep the standards high and work hard as a team.

- **Major Changes or Small Details?**

  Great coaches know to look at the details and take a step-by-step approach when they first take over a program. They consider whether small detail adjustments can create a significant difference or if a big overhaul is needed. Change a bad situation by making the most influential major change first, observing and analyzing the effects, and then continuing while in a good program. Look to the details (smaller changes) to improve upon what is already good.

- **Maintain a Balance**

  This is possibly the most important tip: Creating balance is the only way to lead a great life. You can achieve success without balance, but you cannot be a great leader. Contrary to what many preach, being single-minded is not the best approach since it means overlooking your health, family, and community—all of which will help you become a better leader to your team, business, and organization.

It's a cop out to say that you must solely focus on one goal and ignore the other aspects of your life. Finding the balance between your priorities makes each aspect better as you put your energy, creativity, and passion into your health, family, community, and program (or work).

ACKNOWLEDGEMENTS _____

I chose to write this book to share my experiences with other coaches and leaders in the hope that an idea sticks with them and helps them along their journey. The trail for me was mostly a joyous one that I felt lucky to be on. The start of my gratitude began with my family. Growing up, my family was always involved in sports, whether it was watching, playing, or simply talking about sports. It was part of our everyday life. I am thankful to my dad, Leon, mom, Katie, brother, Don, and sisters, Betsy and Karen, who created a home where sports—and the lessons from sports—were emphasized.

Continuing chronologically, the coaches I had as a youth and young adult made a significant impact on how important sports were for me and why I wanted to be a coach someday. These coaches included Leon K., Grover H., Tom F., Jimmy W., Charles P., and Jim P. They led with passion and taught lifelong lessons that carried into my coaching throughout my career.

My college and local teammates motivated me to learn more about soccer. They saw that I was always willing to run and win the ball because of my work ethic and pure love of the game. I wasn't as technically gifted as the players who had more formal training, but I pride myself on never giving up. My teammates elected me captain as a living example of the decisions that should be made on and off the field. Their appreciation made me work even harder at being fit and being a ball winner for our team, which led to my belief that every player can include these qualities in their game, no matter their skill level. This was an important part of the successful teams that I was a member of as a leader. The athletes I played with were a crucial part of my coaching education. I'd like to give a special mention to the following athletes who took extra time to help my passion for soccer grow: Terry W., Scott D., and Chris B.

When Deb and I moved back to Florida, my coaching career began. I could not have done this without support from the junior high and junior college coaches and teachers who have taught me so much along the way: Dave M., Bill W., Wayne M., Harry H., and Charles P.

The athletes and assistant coaches with whom I had the absolute pleasure of building programs at the four-year college level were the most important part of my journey on this trail, besides my immediate family, and I would like to give special shout-outs to a number of them at each stop along this trail.

At USCS, Joe B. and Mim S. were colleagues who helped me understand this institution, along with Tom D. and Jerry B.—two of the best people I worked with as administrators. The chancellor at USCS, Olin S., believed we should have a soccer program. The assistant coaches were Robbie C. and Fred L., with a number of student assistants. The teams I coached at USCS were key to boosting me and our program to an awesome start. The leaders of those teams included Greg S., Bob C., Mario D. P., Jim M., Mathew B., Greg W., Carlos O., Jorge V., Fred L.,

Martin H., Matt H., Paul M., Keith P., J. R. F., and Roger W. I may have forgotten someone, but know if you played on these teams at USCS, you made a huge difference in my career—and in shaping what I believe a team can truly achieve. The cross-country team at USCS also made a difference in what I could expect from myself, as I also coached them with help from Curtis F. The special guys who affected my coaching and running career here were Mike M., David C., Terry O., Pat M., Doug B., Rob W., Skip F., Rocky M., Sherman E., and Martin H. All the runners created a special bond on this team, whether I mentioned your name or not.

UNC Charlotte was our next stop, with again, some talented players making big contributions to extraordinarily successful teams. The administrator that brought me in was Jeff M.—a great leader who has done everything in his sport and was always kind to share his knowledge. Two other special members of the support team were Mark C. and Tom W. They spoiled me in what my expectations were for other sports info or marketing people. The assistants were Jesse M., Sean B., Rick Z., Al P., and Mike V. They helped create a new standard for UNC Charlotte soccer. The leaders and captains who were key to the success of the program included: Ricky R. G., Bobby R., Gabe G., Aidan H., Carlos G., Ant R., Bart M., Randy S., Shawn K., Mike R., Darren F., Mac C., Craig A., Jon B., Lance R., Ian D., Richard S., John C., and Kevin F. This was a team that showed a team can have it all when they decide to raise standards and compete everyday.

Along the way, I also got to work with a couple of special Olympic Development Program teams in North

Carolina and Colorado, and those experiences continued my growth and creativity. I got to coach alongside Elmar B., Wolfgang S., Karem D., and Marcelo B., as these teams found regional and national success. These programs gave me the chance to work with some exceptionally talented players in a tournament atmosphere. These teams, athletes, and coaches helped me gain experience in taking underdog teams to success.

The two professional experiences with the Raleigh Flyers and Richmond Kickers helped me experience working with professional athletes, professional owners, and staff. Special gratitude here to Ray G., Jim G., and Louis G. I learned some ideas about man (player) management and dealing with where to put my trust. I also gained a lifelong friend with Tim H., who provided me with other learning opportunities. I'm happy that both teams made their respective playoffs but learned that sometimes areas out of your control change outcomes.

A couple of others who were helping factors along the journey for many years were Eric V., David P., and Dr. Dano. They provided good counsel and support at many trailheads along the way.

At Colorado School of Mines, I have to thank the athletes, coaches, and administrators who helped change that program into a national and regional power. The coaches included Kevin F., Greg M., Hank L., Lori S., Yan D., Lindsey S., and Izzy A. The leaders and captains were John B., Jason H., Craig T., Joe H., Tesho A., Chike S., Blasko, Diane W., Pocket Rocket, Zona, Nico D., Marc M., Eric T., Jimmy T., Robbie W., Travis F., Jared P., Jay M., Justin C., Joel F., Sean R.K., O. J. B., Justin B., Mike D., Rafael R., Daniel

L., Brian L., Mac H., Nick K., Kevin G., Jason D., Zach K., John M., Nao L., Cam B., Grant M., Trevor B., Phil W., Jacob J., Chris B., Cale H., Manville S., Alex G., Alex N., Jeff N., Baski B., Nic A., Giuseppe P., Tannor R., Dre R., Richard G., Zach P. B., Chayce M., Seun O., Jared H., Rado, Niki G., David B., John H., Liz M., Mikayla B., Corrine J., Ann N., Allison H., Liz O., Kelsey L., Jess S., Adrea J., Stef F., and Dani H. The administrators who were key to building a successful program at Mines and helped me a great deal were Marv K., and Tom S. All these and others were key to being a part of the shaping of extraordinary programs at CSM.

Part of continuing my growth as a coach was the 17 years I was part of the leadership team at Real Colorado Soccer with Lorne D., Ken W., Jared S., Theresa E., and Flanny. This group, and many volunteers and athletes, helped Lorne build this youth club from underdogs to dawgs on a national level. Also, again, it was part of finding creative ways to win and then continuing to push standards.

After coaching at Mines, there were a number of people who helped in building Best Day Ever Consulting: Ross D., Tim S., Graeme J., Robbie C., Shane C., and Dr. Dano. The opportunity to become the head coach at the University of Central Arkansas comes with a special thanks for this opportunity to Ross D., Houston D., and Brad T. The athletes who were captains and leaders at UCA were Jerry G., Kevin V., Alex K., Sohma I., Pietro F., Josh B. The assistant coaches who helped us continue to change the culture were Kyle S., Chase R., Rosey, Matt T., Will M., Niklas B., and Travis C.

I also have gratitude to the coaches whom I got to compete against in conferences, such as NAIA District 6, Metro Conference, Sun Belt Conference, RMAC, and ASUN. Playing against better coaches who've built strong teams always makes you develop to a higher level.

Some friends have been a part of supporting us and an integral part for several decades in this journey, including Mark H., Sue H., Bill M., Maggie M., Amanda H., and Marcus H. My friends at Nike, Joe E., Ed A., Raf O., Russell P., and Em M. helped me everywhere I coached.

Helping greatly to put this book together were Emily M. and Maddie C. Thank you for helping get my ideas across and making all our author meetings worth looking forward to as enjoyable experiences.

Finally, the most credit for aiding me on this trail less travelled is Deb and our 13 dogs and 9 cats, who were all glad to see me, no matter the result of the day's match. They had the ability to make me feel like today was a special day and that tomorrow would be another gift.

What will tomorrow's gift be? I can't be sure, but it may include getting to advise some other leaders, programs, or coaches. What I do know is that it will surely be cherished with Deb in Golden, Colorado, or wherever our journey takes us!

Former University of Central Arkansas head coach of men's soccer, Ross Duncan, and I discuss tactics on the sidelines during a consulting session.

Enjoying the sunset at UCA with Ross.

The team at the University of South Carolina Spartanburg stands with the District 6 Trophy in 1983.

A USCS team picture after our match vs. Clemson in 1983. It ended as a 1–1 draw. Clemson was ranked #1 in the nation as a DI program, and USCS was ranked #1 in the NAIA.

UNC Charlotte team picture in 1989.
My first year coaching at Charlotte.

UCA after their 1–0 victory over Missouri State in 2017,
when I served as a team consultant.

The 2021 UCA team enjoying time on Jacksonville Beach.

Me and the 2023 UCA team volunteering at the
Foothills Animal Shelter in Colorado.

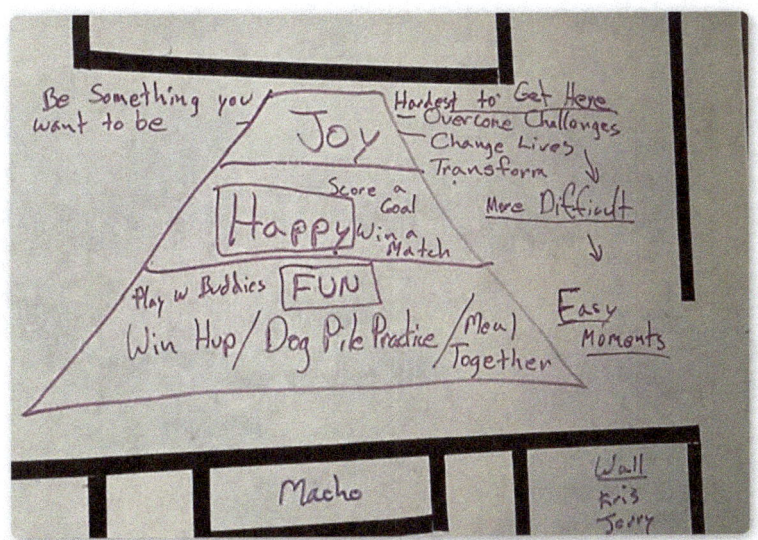

Be Something you / Hardest to Get Here
want to be — Overcome Challenges
JOY — Change Lives
— Transform

Score a
Goal More Difficult
Happy Win a
Match

Play w Buddies FUN Easy
Win Hop / Dog Pile Practice /Mew Moments
Together

Macho Wall
Kris
Jerry

My "Pyramid of Joy" drawing in the team locker room.

Daja and I during the UCA athletics media
day session. The unofficial, official mascot.

Daja as the superstar she is during the UCA
athletics media day.

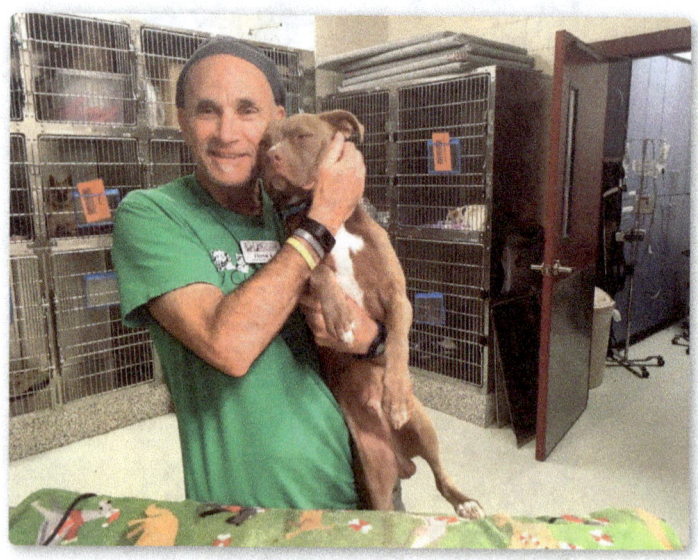

My four-legged friend (Frank) and I at the Foothills Animal
Shelter, before he was adopted in Golden, Colorado.

My beautiful wife and I attending a fundraiser.

Daja looking over the week's plan with me in Conway, Arkansas.

Me consulting the CSU Monterey Bay Otters in 2019
with Coach Graeme Jaap.

The Colorado School of Mines men's soccer team photo
after winning the RMAC Championship in 2011.

The Colorado School of Mines men's soccer team hoisting the Rocky Mountain Athletic Conference trophy in 2015.

Winners of the West Florida Tournament with the Purple United summer team in 1976. That's me, with a lot more hair, holding the cup on the right.

Former players of mine, Mac Cozier (left) and Jon Busch (right), and I at Mile High Stadium 2 in 1997. Both athletes are in UNC Charlotte's Athletics Hall of Fame. Mac played for the Columbus Crew in the MLS, and Jon played for the United States Men's National Soccer Team.